DATE			

How the Sun Made a Promise and Kept It

How the Sun Made a Promise and Kept It

A Canadian Indian Myth

retold by

Margery Bernstein & Janet Kobrin

illustrated by

Ed Heffernan

Charles Scribner's Sons, New York

To
EDGAR BERNSTEIN
and
PHILIP MONTAG
whose talents created the Independent
Learning Project, and whose support and
enthusiasm made this book possible.

How the Sun Made a Promise and Kept It was first told by the
Bungee or Swampy Indians of Lake Winnipeg in central Canada.

LONG, long ago, the god Weese-ke-jak made the earth and the sky. There were oceans and lakes. There was dry land.

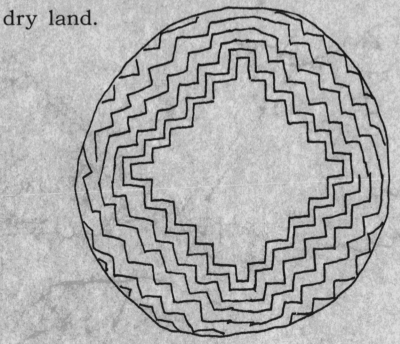

Weese-ke-jak made birds to fly in the sky. He made fish to swim in the oceans and lakes. He made animals to live on the land.

The earth was a beautiful place. But sometimes it was not a good place to live.

In those days, the sun went wherever he wanted to go. He only visited the earth sometimes. When he was away it was dark and cold.

"I must do something," thought Weese-ke-jak. "We need the sun to light and warm us."

Weese-ke-jak thought and thought. At last he had a plan.

"The next time the sun visits the earth,"
Weese-ke-jak said, "I will catch him in a
net. I will keep him close to the earth.
Then the earth will always be warm and
light."

10

Weese-ke-jak made a net out of ropes.

The net was very large and very strong.

Then Weese-ke-jak waited.

When the sun came near the earth
again, Weese-ke-jak took his net. He
swung it around and around. Then he
threw it up into the sky.

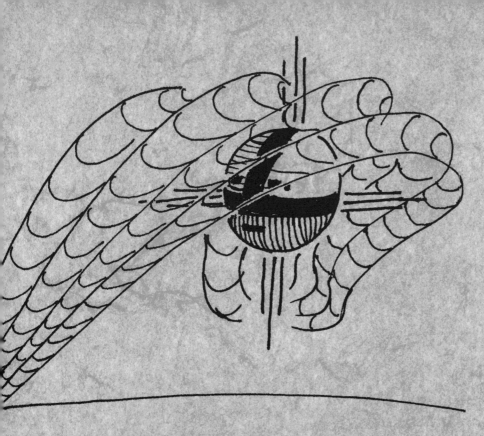

The net dropped over the sun.

The sun was caught!

Weese-ke-jak pulled the sun in the net down toward the earth. He tied the ropes to a tree stump.

The sun pushed and pulled. But he could not free himself.

"Let me go, Weese-ke-jak," begged the sun. "Let me go! Why do you keep me in this net?"

"I have trapped you so that I can keep you near the earth," answered Weese-ke-jak. "Now the earth will be warm and light all the time."

And Weese-ke-jak
would not let the sun go.

But Weese-ke-jak had made a great mistake! He had pulled the sun too near the earth.

It began to get hotter and hotter. Soon it was so hot that the birds flew down out of the sky to see what had happened. The animals came out of the forests.

"If it gets any hotter," thought Weese-ke-jak, "everything will begin to burn. I must let the sun out of the net. Maybe I can make him promise not to go too far away."

Then Weese-ke-jak called
to the sun.

"I feel sorry for you and
I might let you go.
But you must promise
something."

22

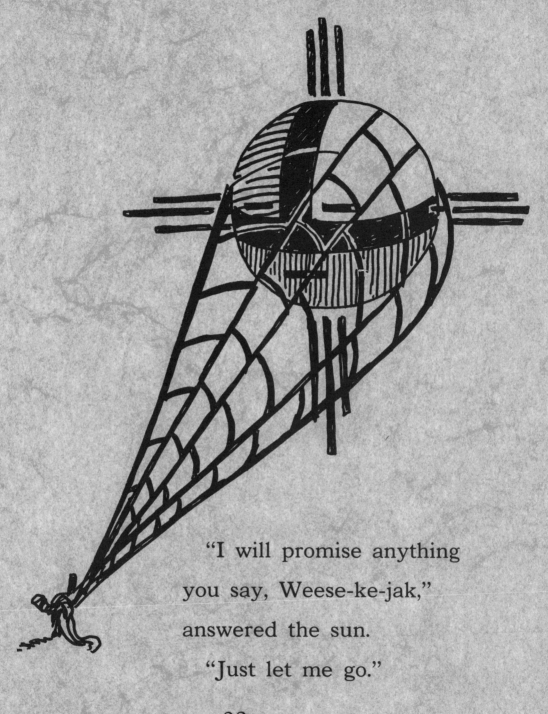

"I will promise anything
you say, Weese-ke-jak,"
answered the sun.
"Just let me go."

"Well..." said Weese-ke-jak. He
pretended to think about it. "Will you
keep your promise?"

He pretended that he still wasn't sure he
should let the sun go.

"I *will* keep my promise," cried the sun.
"What must I do?"

"You must never go too far away," said Weese-ke-jak. "You may come close to the edges of the earth, but only in the morning and in the evening. During the day you must come just near enough to warm the earth."

25

"I will do as you say," said the sun.
"Now, please let me go!"

Weese-ke-jak went over to free the sun.
But it was so hot that he could not get
near the net.

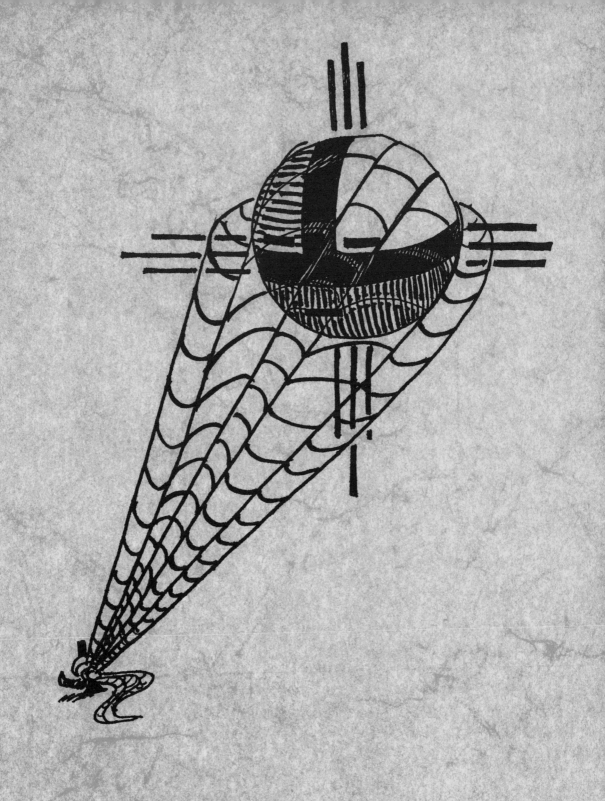

So Weese-ke-jak called to the animals.

"I cannot get close to the sun," he said. "Can anyone help me?"

A few of the animals were brave. They tried to help Weese-ke-jak.

First, Deer tried to free the sun. Then Fox tried. Then Otter tried. They could not come near enough. It was too hot.

Then Beaver came.

"I will try," he said.

In those days, Beaver did not look like
he does now. He had only a few small
teeth. His fur was rough and prickly. He
was not very handsome. But he was
brave.

Beaver ran to the net. He quickly began
to bite the ropes that held the net.

It was very, very hot. But Beaver did
not give up.

At last, Beaver bit through the last rope.

The sun was free! It rose up from the

earth like a balloon.

The earth became cooler.

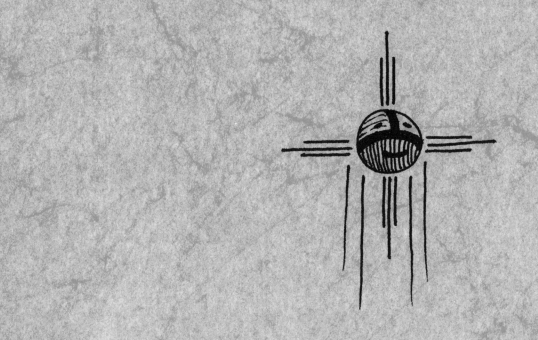

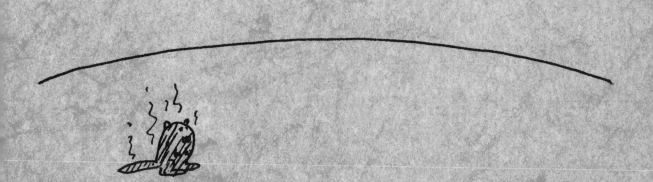

Weese-ke-jak and the animals were
happy. They ran to thank Beaver.

Poor Beaver! He was not happy. The
heat from the sun had ruined his coat. He
had almost no fur left.

"Don't be unhappy, Beaver," said
Weese-ke-jak. "Because you were so brave
I will give you two gifts."

Weese-ke-jak gave Beaver a new coat.
The fur was smooth and soft. He gave
Beaver a new set of fine sharp teeth.

But Weese-ke-jak did not put any fur on Beaver's tail.

"Beaver's tail will always be bare," said Weese-ke-jak, "so everyone will remember how brave he was. They will remember that he set the sun free."

As for the sun, although he was free
from the earth, he was not free from
Weese-ke-jak's net. It still hangs over him.

Look carefully at the sun in the morning
or in the evening when it is close to the
earth. Look and you will see the long
ropes hanging from the sun. The ropes
remind the sun of his promise to
Weese-ke-jak.

And in all the days of the world since
then, the sun has kept this promise.